Blue Skies

Blue Skies

FRESH ADVICE ABOUT LIFE FROM FIRST GRADERS

Written by the First Graders in Room 104 at The Potter's House

Photography by Beth Vander Kolk

credo
house publishers

All rights reserved.
Published in the United States by Credo House Publishers,
a division of Credo Communications, LLC, Grand Rapids, Michigan.
www.credocommunications.net

Published in partnership with The Potter's House.

The Potter's House mission is to provide a Christ-centered education
to children of all ethnic heritages and income levels, equipping them
to serve God and society to their fullest potential.

To respond to the message of this book, for more information about the
school, and for details on how to order additional copies of Blue Skies,
please contact us at

The Potter's House
810 Van Raalte Dr SW
Grand Rapids, MI 49509

Email: cbeals@pottershouseschool.org
World Wide Web: www.pottershouseschool.org

Compiled by Beth Vander Kolk
Designed by Sharon VanLoozenoord

ISBN-13: 978-0-9787620-5-6
ISBN-10: 0-9787620-5-3

Printed in the United States of America

10 9 8 7 6 5 4 3 2 1

First Edition

This project is dedicated to our families and friends.

Thank you for your encouragement and support.

A special thanks goes to all those involved in the Ele:Vate economic literacy initiative.

You have equipped us to choose well.

This 2006-2007 first-grade class taught by Miss Beth Vander Kolk

attends The Potter's House school in Grand Rapids, Michigan.

www.pottershouseschool.org

The Potter's House

An Urban, Christ-Centered School

Contents

Advice About

Getting Dressed

Remember to have everything on before
you go outside. —Rebecca

Never dress in front of an open window.

—Logan

Never wear your swimsuit in the winter
because you will freeze. —Elijah

It is a good idea to get help picking out your clothes when you are confused. —Miguel

Always make sure that your clothes match or people may laugh at you. —Anthony

Look for the things that you want to wear early in the morning so that you have enough time to find them. —Zachary

Always set all of your clothes out next to you
before you get dressed or you might not
know where they are. —Emily

If you take a bath everyday before you
get dressed it will take three hours to get
ready. —Jasmine

Always get dressed fast when it is cold out.
—Indira

Always wear high-heeled shoes when you
go to the mall. —Tatyana

Always put your shirt on before your pants
so it won't get squished. —Hailey

Don't wear really nice clothes if you are about
to get dirty. —Joshua

Never put on people's clothes without asking them first. —Destiny

Never wear your brother's clothes if they are too big for you. —Dakari

Never put on clothes that could fall off easily. —William

Advice About
Eating

Always use good manners when a guest comes over or they may be sad when they leave. —Jasmine

Never chew food in your mouth and then show it to people. They will think that you are messy. —Cassie

Never put your face in your food. It will make your company feel uncomfortable inside. —Hannah

Don't eat like a pig. It is disrespectful. —Zachary

Always put your napkin on your lap or it will end
up on top of your food. —Nathan

Never play with your food or it could
end up on your pants. —Rebecca

Always wash your hands before you eat or you could get your food dirty. —Caleb

Never eat too fast or you could get dizzy. —Logan

Always cook your food before you eat it or it will be stone cold. —Hailey

Always put the right ingredients into whatever food you make or you might get sick and die. —Rayona

Never eat something that you are not supposed to. Especially if you are a vegetarian. —Joshua

Never eat poison ivy. —William

Never cut up your spaghetti. —Indira

The best food is macaroni. You need
to chew it at least five times. —Anthony

The best restaurants have a lot of people
in them. —Destiny

Advice About

Cleaning the House

Always make your bed before company comes over because you want them to think that you are neat. —Hailey

Never stuff things under your bed or you might get in trouble. —Jasmine

Keep the living room clean so you can take a nap there. —Rodney

Never scare little kids with your vacuum. —Kate

Never suck up the wrong things with a vacuum.

—Hannah

Vacuum up dog fur once a day or you might end up eating some. —Nyrese

Always wash your dog in the bathtub so you won't make a mess. —Zachary

Always use a blue broom when you are cleaning the bathroom. —AnaLee

Never use a wet mop on the carpet. It might smoosh the dirt into it. —Logan

Never leave stuff lying on the floor. You may lose it forever. —William

Always keep your room clean so you don't hurt yourself. —Joshua

Always pick up your toys when you are done with them or you may have to sit alone in your room. —Anthony

Never go into the house with muddy shoes.

—Nathan

Never hold your juice glass with a wet hand.

—Rebecca

Always smell everything before you put it back in the refrigerator. —Tatyana

advice about

Safety

Never push someone on the sidewalk when they are wearing a long dress. —Rebecca

Always watch for cars when you are on the sidewalk. —Hannah

Be careful when you are selling cookie dough. People could yell at you. —Rayona

Never talk to bad-looking strangers. —Miguel

Always run away from strange dogs. —Indira

Always lock the doors of your house at night so that people won't bother you.

—Dakari

Never look up when a squirrel is gathering acorns. —Logan

Always make sure that you are a good climber before you go up in a tree. —William

Always tie your shoes before going to gym class. —Emily

Never stick a bead up your nose. —Destiny

Never stand up when you are in a fire.

—Rodney

Always wear your sunglasses when it is hot
so that your eyes won't burn. —Tatyana

Always charge up your cell phone before you go in the woods. —Elijah

If you get struck by lightening, you should get to the hospital fast. —Nathan

Don't go outside by yourself. —AnaLee

Advice About

Driving

Always keep your eyes on the front window.

—William

Don't look at the people that are riding with you. —Indira

Never close your eyes while you are driving because you might get a ticket or go to jail.

—Rayona

Never play games while you are driving, even if you are getting a high score. —Elijah

When you are driving on a busy street, make sure that you go straight ahead. —Joshua

Don't drink while you are stopped at a red light or you may spill on your pants.

—Hailey

Never let go of the steering wheel or the car will go wherever it wants. —Rodney

Always keep quiet in your car or you will get out of control. —Caleb

Clean your car once in a while. If it gets too dirty, it doesn't work well. —Hannah

Never stand up when you are driving. —Kate

Never open the door when you are driving fast. —Hannah

Always have your seat belt on when you are driving so you won't fly out of your car. —Cassie

Never drive too fast on your driveway. —Nathan

Never smoke while you are driving because you could freeze in the winter with the window open. —Logan

Always park your car on the side of the street so wacky drivers won't hit it. —Anthony

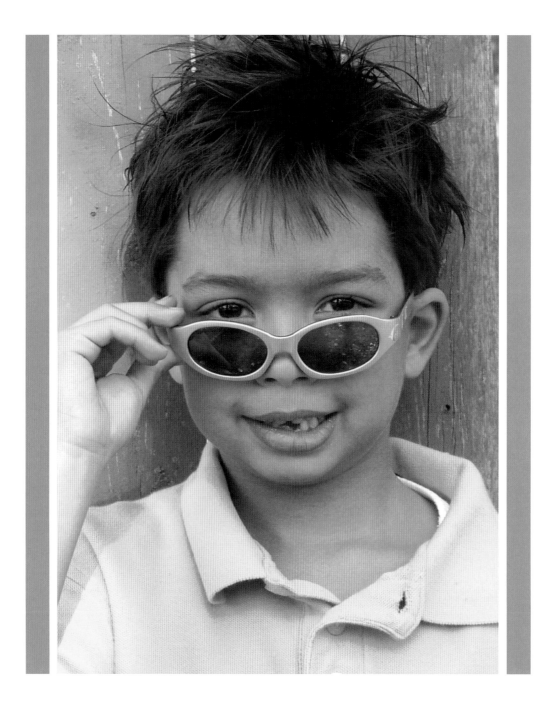

Advice About

Getting and Keeping a Job

Think about what you are smart at and
do that. —Hailey

Have your dad teach you all that he knows
and then learn some more. —Anthony

Practice a lot so that you can be good
at your job. —Destiny

Ask how much money you will get paid. You want a job that makes a lot of money. —Logan

Get a hard job. They pay more. —AnaLee

Get two jobs. One for money and the other for fun. —Nyrese

Get to your job on time and work fast or you might not get all of your work done. —Rayona

If you do your job on roller skates, you'll be faster. —Zachary

Never make a mess at work. —Emily

Never do something that your boss didn't say or you won't get paid. —Hannah

Always do your job right because it will make your boss happy. —William

Try to listen and then you will get stuff done right. —Joshua

Help the other people at work if they can't do stuff by themselves. —Caleb

Never let the machines run out of batteries.
—Rodney

Get a job that lets you have your own computer. —Dakari

Help the other people at work if they can't do stuff by themselves. —Caleb

Never let the machines run out of batteries.

—Rodney

Get a job that lets you have your own computer. —Dakari

Advice About Shopping

Always take a lot of money with you. —Hailey

Always pay for things before you leave the store. —Destiny

Never leave something on the floor if you are not going to buy it. —Rodney

Never run while you are shopping. —Rebecca

Always look straight ahead when you are
pushing your cart. —Kate

Watch out for other shoppers or you
might run into them. —Dakari

Always look where you are going in a store or you might knock down boxes. —Emily

Don't kick the bread. —Nathan

Always make sure that your vegetables are good before you buy them or they might make you sick. —Rayona

Don't beg for too much stuff or you may end up with nothing. —Anthony

Only buy the things that you need to get. —Zachary

Don't buy anything that is too expensive because you will spend too much of your money and you won't have enough later when you need it. —Joshua

Try on a lot of clothes before you buy any. —Indira

Always buy the right size or you won't use it.

—Jasmine

Never get lost in a parking lot. It may
be hard for people to find you. —Cassie

Advice About

Getting Married

Always marry a handsome guy so you will want to keep him. —Tatyana

Don't marry someone that you really don't like or you may fight. —Joshua

Make sure that you marry a smart person. If you don't things can get out of control.
—Anthony

Wait until you grow up to get married. —Nyrese

Never marry somebody over ninety because
they won't last very long. —Logan

Always let your partner know before
you get married. —William

Always buy your wedding gown at least a week before your wedding or you may have to cancel. —Hailey

Get married in a red dress because it is the most popular. —Jasmine

Always get dressed up when you get married because it is important. —Dakari

Always have the wedding before you have
the party. —Caleb

Never run down the aisle when you get
married. —Cassie

Never yell out when the preacher is talking
at a wedding. —Destiny

Never laugh in front of people when they kiss at their wedding. —Rebecca

If you are getting married, don't say, "Eeeww, I don't want to kiss you." —Rodney

I have no idea about that. —Zachary

Advice About

Caring For Kids

Make sure that you have a good babysitter.

—Emily

When your kids are born, buy them some math toys so they can get smart. —Rayona

Always take your turn burping the baby.

—Nathan

Always wear a bib when you are burping the baby. —AnaLee

Rock your baby to sleep by rocking around the house to low music. —Elijah

Hold your baby quietly when they are crying. —Tatyana

Catch your kids when they try to run in the
street. —Miguel

Never let kids use matches or they might
burn their eye. —Logan

Always keep your kids inside when it is super
cold outside. —Anthony

Never let your kids scream in the hallway.
The neighbors might hear them. —Rodney

Always help your kids with their homework.
It makes them happier. —Zachary

Always put your kids to bed on time or they will
be too tired when they wake up. —Caleb

Give your child a bath every day because kids can get sticky. —Hailey

Feed your kids a lot of pizza. —Dakari

Never let your kids fight with their food or you will get a big mess. —Nyrese

Advice About

Getting Along With Your Family

Always talk things out when you are making a decision. —Rodney

Make sure that you say that you are sorry when you do something wrong. —Joshua

Pay attention to everyone. —Anthony

Always do what your parents say or you may get into trouble. —Logan

Never say bad words to your mom or dad because they are grown ups. —Jasmine

Make pictures for your mom and dad. It makes them surprised. —Zachary

Never throw toys at your brothers or else
they will tell on you. —Caleb

Never squish cake in your sister's face. It isn't
pretty. (Trust me. I tried it once.) —Hannah

Always help your sister make the bed or she'll
be mad. —Hailey

If you sleep with someone, don't steal the covers. —Destiny

Never hit your dog or it will make him mad. —Nyrese

Make sure that you relax together after you clean the house. —Tatyana

Eat ice cream together. It will cool you down.

—Elijah

Have a family party with a piñata. It makes people happy. —AnaLee

Play football together because hitting in football isn't against the rules.

—Nathan

Advice About

Helping a Friend

Always stop and help your friend if they fall down in a race, even if you know that you are not going to win. —Rebecca

Always help your friend when other people are giving them trouble. —Nyrese

If you have a friend, you should pay attention to them and other people. —Anthony

Cupcakes, cakes, and pies will make your friend happy. —Jasmine

If your friend is in a bad mood, you could surprise them with a little gift. —Rayona

Always say thank you when your friends are nice to you. —Caleb

A good way to make friends is to help them clean their bedroom. —Zachary

Always help your friend pick up the toys. —Emily

If you find anything that belongs to your friend, make sure that you give it back. —Destiny

Never shove your friend off of their bike.

—Rodney

Call an ambulance if your friend is ever hurt.

—William

Always help your friend with their band-aids.

—Miguel

Always play with your best friend when you go to a birthday party. —Hailey

Never tell your friends that they are ugly.

—Hannah

Take your friend to the office when they are feeling sick. —AnaLee

Advice About

Going on Vacation

Always pack the stuff that you want to
play with first so you will make sure that you
have it. —Anthony

Always bring your own place to sleep
or else you will get very cold sleeping
outside. —Kate

Always pack your favorite clothes so you
will be comfortable. —Joshua

Always bring your swimsuit when you go camping, otherwise you will have to swim in your clothes. —Cassie

Be careful when you go out into deep water.

—Rebecca

Never kick sand in people's faces when you are at the beach. —Rodney

If it is a long trip, make sure that you sleep

in the car. —Zachary

Never take your dog when you fly on an

airplane. It will make the other people mad.

—Logan

Always pack your own food because it is

the best. —Nyrese

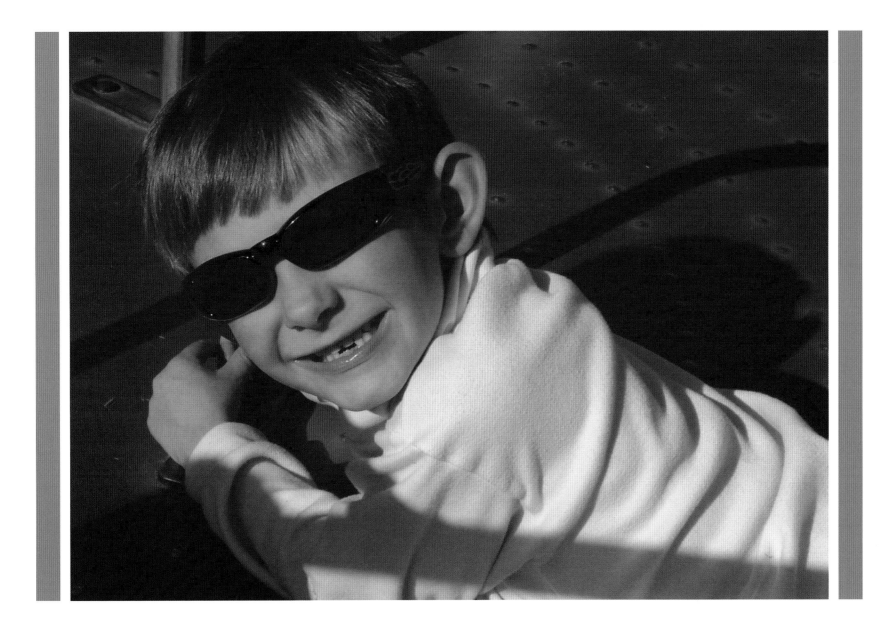

Never make your parents worried by running
off somewhere. —Rayona

Never take robbers with you on vacation
because they will give you trouble. —William

Never go somewhere that is too dangerous
for your children. —Joshua

Always go on vacation with the people you love. —Dakari

Don't take too much stuff with you or it will take you a really long time to unpack. —Tatyana

The best place to go on vacation is at your own home. —Indira

Advice About

Getting Ready for Bed

Always wear something comfortable to bed
or you may be up all night. —Joshua

Cozy pajamas are the best. —Kate

Flowered pajamas help you sleep better.
—Jasmine

Always keep your promises before you go to bed.

—Rayona

Brush your teeth before you put on your pajamas because otherwise you might forget. —Cassie

Always sing Happy Birthday twice while you are brushing your teeth. —Hannah

Don't argue about your bed time. —Nyrese

Never play around while you are getting

dressed for bed. —Rodney

Never take your socks off before you go to bed.

—Miguel

Never watch scary stuff on TV before you go to bed. —Tatyana

Make sure that you set your timer before you go to bed. —Hailey

If anyone is sleeping, don't jump on the bed. —Destiny

Always close your eyes when you go to bed.
It will help you sleep. —Nathan

Always read one or two chapters in bed. It will
help you fall asleep faster. —Emily

If you talk about animals before you go
to sleep, you will have good dreams.
—Indira

Contributors

List of students in alphabetical order according to their last name.

AnaLee	Indira
Rayona	Destiny
Elijah	Hailey
Rodney	Hannah
Joshua	Caleb
Nyrese	William
Tatyana	Zachary
Miguel	Jasmine
Logan	Anthony
Kate	Nathan
Emily	Dakari
Rebecca	Cassie